The
Exxon Valdez
1989:

An oil tanker runs aground

JOHN TOWNSEND

Raintree

www.raintreepublishers.co.uk

Visit our website to find out more information about **Raintree** books.

To order:
- ☎ Phone 44 (0) 1865 888113
- 🖹 Send a fax to 44 (0) 1865 314091
- 💻 Visit the Raintree bookshop at **www.raintreepublishers.co.uk** to browse our catalogue and order online.

First published in Great Britain by Raintree, Halley Court, Jordan Hill, Oxford OX2 8EJ, part of Harcourt Education.

Raintree is a registered trademark of Harcourt Education Ltd.

Editorial: Andrew Farrow and Richard Woodham
Design: Victoria Bevan and AMR Design Ltd
Illustrations: David Woodroffe
Picture Research: Maria Joannou and Ginny Stroud-Lewis
Production: Helen McCreath

Originated by Modern Age
Printed and bound in China by South China Printing Company

10 digit ISBN 1 406 20292 4
13 digit ISBN 978 1 406 20292 2
10 09 08 07 06
10 9 8 7 6 5 4 3 2 1

British Library Cataloguing in Publication Data
Townsend, John
The Exxon Valdez, 1989. - (When disaster struck)
363.7'382'09798
A full catalogue record for this book is available from the British Library.

Acknowledgements
The publishers would like to thank the following for permission to reproduce photographs: Anchorage Daily News pp.12, 38; Corbis pp.4 (Danny Lehman), 14 (Bettmann), 15 (Natalie Fobes), 16 (Natalie Fobes), 17 (Natalie Fobes), 18 (Natalie Fobes), 26 (Natalie Fobes), 27 (Gary Braasch), 28, 33 (Natalie Fobes), 35 (Natalie Fobes), 47 (Natalie Fobes), 49; Empics pp.22 (Rob Stapleton/AP), 23 (John Gaps III/AP), 36 (Al Grillo/AP), 40 (Al Grillo/AP), 45 (John Gaps III/AP); Getty Images pp.8 (National Geographic/ George F Herben), 9 (The Image Bank/Harald Sund), 24 (AFP), 32 (AFP), 48 (Photodisc); Getty Images News pp.39, 42, 44, 46; Mirrorpix p.21; Photolibrary.com p.10; Science Photo Library p.29 (Vanessa Vick).

Cover photograph of workers using hot-water hoses and pump machinery to wash oil-coated rocks, reproduced with permission of Science Photo Library (Vanessa Vick).

The publishers would like to thank Richard Dworsky and Carolyn Rosner for their assistance in the preparation of this book.

Every effort has been made to contact copyright holders of any material reproduced in this book. Any omissions will be rectified in subsequent printings if notice is given to the publishers.

The paper used to print this book comes from sustainable resources.

CONTENTS

Any words appearing in the text in bold, **like this**, are explained in the glossary.

AN OIL TANKER RUNS AGROUND

The *Exxon Valdez, 1989*

MORNING NEWS

At first it seemed like just another short story at the end of the news.

The voice on the radio calmly added:

"We are just receiving reports of an oil tanker in difficulty off the coast of Alaska. The supertanker Exxon Valdez *has apparently struck a rock. She is carrying crude oil from the port of Valdez in Alaska to ports around the United States. The captain is reported to have sent a distress message soon after midnight. He stated the vessel had run aground and was leaking oil. So far we have no further information. We will keep you informed of any further developments."*

There were many further developments. At first there seemed little to worry about. It sounded like a minor accident. But that night in 1989 has gone down in history as one of the worst **environmental** disasters of all time.

The *Exxon Valdez* ran aground in Prince William Sound, shown here.

WAITING TO
HAPPEN

The *Exxon Valdez, 1989*

Bering
Sea

ALASKA

CANADA

0   100   200 Miles
0   100   200 Kilometres

Anchorage   Valdez

*Prince William
Sound*

N

Gulf of Alaska

Kodiak
Island

ALASKA'S OIL

Without oil the modern world would grind to a halt very quickly.

Oil is used to power cars and aeroplanes. It is also used in power stations to make electricity. The United States uses more oil than any other country. After Saudi Arabia and Russia, the United States is the third largest producer of oil. Around 20 per cent of that oil comes from Alaska. Alaska is thought to have the largest underground **oil field** in North America.

Apart from its oil, Alaska is famous for being one of the most beautiful and unspoilt places on Earth. Very few people live there because of the cold winters. Scientists visit to study its mountains, rivers, glaciers, plants, and rich wildlife.

Valdez is the most northern ice-free port in North America.

THE JOURNEY BEGINS

On 23 March 1989, the supertanker *Exxon Valdez* was filled with oil at Valdez. Owned by the Exxon Shipping Company, the huge steel ship was filled with about 200 million litres (53 million gallons) of oil.

Oil from the trans-Alaska pipeline is loaded on to tankers at Valdez to be shipped to refineries on the west coast of the United States.

Shortly after 9:00 p.m., the ship began to edge out of port. The ship was heading for California and this was the ship's 28th voyage.

The captain of the *Exxon Valdez* was 43-year-old Joseph Hazelwood. He watched from the **bridge** as the huge tanker moved slowly out into the darkness of Prince William Sound.

Icy shapes floated on the water. The captain sent a radio message to the coastguard. He said that he would be changing course to leave the shipping lane – the route that ships usually used. He needed to avoid a few small icebergs drifting into the sound. Before going to his cabin around midnight, Captain Hazelwood told his **third mate**, Gregory Cousins, to steer back into the shipping lane. They would be back on course once they passed Busby Island – or so Hazelwood thought.

Gregory Cousins gave instructions to the **helmsman**, Robert Kagan, to steer the *Exxon Valdez* to the right. It is possible that Cousins gave the order too late, or that the helmsman did not respond in time. It may have been that the ship's steering was faulty, or that the captain was confused or drunk. Whatever the reason, the tanker did not turn sharply enough. It was set on a collision course towards underwater rocks.

Just 3 hours after setting sail, and 40 kilometres (25 miles) from Valdez, disaster struck. Suddenly the ship shook and groaned. Its hull scraped over Bligh **Reef** with a judder. The great tanker had **grounded**, and punctured eight of its eleven cargo tanks. The captain ran from his cabin and returned to the bridge. He could not believe what he saw.

THE EXXON VALDEZ

Displacement:
214,862 metric tons
(211,469 tons)

Length:
300 metres (984 feet)

Speed:
16.25 knots
(30 km/h (19 mph))

Cargo Capacity:
235 million litres
(62 million gallons)

ALARM

"WE'RE LEAKING OIL"

"We've fetched up hard aground. We're leaking oil. We're going to be here for a while."
Captain Hazelwood,
12:26 a.m.

The huge tanker was unable to move from the reef.

Captain Hazelwood said that when the tanker hit the reef he knew "something was wrong... pretty seriously wrong". He rushed to find out what had happened and gave orders to the crew to assess the damage. Oil was bubbling up on the **starboard** side of the ship. He did not want to sound the alarm, which might cause panic. It took about 20 minutes before he finally called the coastguard in Valdez to report that they were stuck on rocks. The captain's voice was very slow and strangely calm. He made it sound like a minor accident.

He later said, "There was a good chunk of fear, but I'd better not panic." However, he knew right away this was serious and they were in deep trouble.

For more than 90 minutes the crew tried to move the tanker off the reef. After the first impact, they kept the *Exxon Valdez* charging ahead under full power for more than 13 minutes. Then they cut the power to half speed ahead, then slow ahead, dead slow ahead, and finally stop, all in less than a minute. From 12:20 a.m. to 12:35 a.m. the ship just rested there, creaking.

According to the **ship's log**, the captain then tried to wiggle the ship forwards to get off the reef. During the next hour, he ordered bursts of power and sharp turning of the **rudder** from left to right. But the huge tanker would not move. Captain Hazelwood gave up trying to move the *Exxon Valdez* at 1:45 a.m. on 24 March. He finally ordered the engines to be stopped. There was nothing more the crew could do other than watch helplessly as the oil beneath them flowed into the sea.

Within 4 hours, nearly 27 million litres (7 million gallons) had escaped. But there were still about 208 million litres (55 million gallons) on board. This was more serious than anyone had first thought. Something had to be done quickly.

THE CAPTAIN'S REACTION

"I tried to pull myself together... I could see oil bubbling fast on the starboard side."

Captain Hazelwood

DISASTER PROFILE:

What?	Oil tanker hits a reef, causing the worst oil spill in US history
Where?	Prince William **Sound**, Alaska, United States
When?	March 1989
Outcome:	The US Oil **Pollution** Act, 1990 (see page 41)
Casualties:	Millions of animals, birds, and fish

THE
NEWS
SPREADS

The *Exxon Valdez*, 1989

DAYLIGHT DAWNS

The sun rose over the ocean on the morning of 24 March 1989.

But in Prince William Sound the waters had turned black, and the air was thick with the stench of oil.

Everyone knew the danger. The oil fumes could explode. The ship could **capsize**. Help was needed quickly to get the remaining oil off the *Exxon Valdez*. Within an hour of the first alarm signal, the port of Valdez was closed to traffic. The rescue tug *Stalwart* set out to the stranded tanker. It took the tug 2 hours to make the 40-kilometre (25-mile) trip to Bligh Reef.

By daylight the oil-spill response team was rushing to get all the clean-up equipment ready. They had to look for it in warehouses and load it on to boats. Workers described the scene early that morning as "frantic".

By early morning, the sea around the *Exxon Valdez* was thick with oil.

THE RESPONSE

Rescue workers ran in all directions to get the right equipment for scooping up oil. **Deep-water skimmers** like huge scoops were buried in sheds under crates and boxes. **Booms** had to be dug out of snow drifts. It took many hours to get everything loaded on to boats. Valuable hours were being lost.

At last a large barge left Valdez at 11:00 a.m. By the time it reached the *Exxon Valdez,* over 12 hours had passed since the tanker had run aground. During all that time oil had been gushing from its ripped tanks.

It was not until evening that a vessel called the *Exxon Baton Rouge,* drew alongside and began to pump oil off the *Exxon Valdez.* By then the **oil slick** covered about 78 square kilometres (30 square miles) south and west of the reef. It stretched like a dark, oozing snake for almost 13 kilometres (8 miles).

DID YOU KNOW?

When oil mixes with cold water, it rises to the surface in thick lumps. The surface is covered with a crust of foul-smelling tar.

A smaller vessel, *Exxon Baton Rouge,* pumped oil out of the leaking tanker.

All through the day, hundreds of experts from all over North America were in contact with the **Alaska Response Team**. Many left whatever they were doing to board the next flight to Alaska. Weather experts also flew in to advise the clean-up team.

Apart from the emergency communications centre in Valdez, a second operations centre was set up 480 kilometres (300 miles) away in Anchorage. Here there were growing concerns about the possible damage to all living things in Prince William Sound. The oil was already spreading quickly.

Marine biologists rushed to the scene. They were not prepared for what they found. Dead fish already littered the shore. Birds hopped about helplessly, their feathers caked with oil. Sea otters feebly tried to lick their filthy fur clean.

Scientists set up a base for cleaning oil from otters. The Bird Research Centre of Berkeley, California, set up a centre to clean oiled birds. The task seemed hopeless. The seeping black poison was already claiming many animals' lives.

Scientists rushed to get the booms ready. The booms were used to try to stop the oil from spreading.

CONSTANT FLOW

On the morning of 25 March, Exxon announced that 28 million litres (7 million gallons) of oil had spilled. By midday the figure reached 41 million litres (11 million gallons). That was nearly 20 per cent of the tanker's cargo, and the oil was still pouring from its gashed hull.

TO THE RESCUE

▷ THE CLEAN-UP BEGINS

"The clean-up is not going well. Believe me, that is an understatement. We have a mess on our hands."

Frank Iarossi, president of the Exxon Shipping Company, on viewing the scene.

The plan was to scoop the oil slick before it reached beaches and spread even further. But the operation started badly. High winds made the operation difficult. The booms that stretched around the slick like a necklace could not contain it all. The US Coast Guard sprayed chemicals in an attempt to break up the sludge. But the scale of the problem was just too great. Where it was safe to do so, emergency crews tried to burn off the layer of oil on the sea itself. The smoke and fumes caused by this added to the chaos.

A boom was placed around the *Exxon Valdez* after the oil spill.

Workers unloaded booms into the water to try to stop more oil spreading across Prince William Sound.

Local people could only watch in horror as the rescue team battled to shrink the slick, but it just kept growing. It was like trying to soak up a river with a few bath-sponges. Fishermen knew that if it was not stopped soon, their whole way of life would be ruined. The other important business in the area was tourism. Tourists came to see the wildlife. Suddenly hundreds of jobs were under threat. Sea ducks and seals were already coated in oil. The scale of the disaster was now becoming clear. The rescue teams had a massive job on their hands and it looked like a hopeless race against time.

A TOUGH JOB

A spokesman for the Alaska department of environment said that efforts to steer the *Valdez* back into the narrow shipping lane were like "trying to park a Cadillac in a Volkswagen spot".

LIMITING THE DAMAGE

The Exxon Valdez, 1989

STEMMING THE FLOW

Before long everyone feared the worst – this was likely to be the largest oil spill in the United States' history.

It was like a massive lake of deadly, oozing sludge, and it was on the move. For many days hundreds of people worked around the clock to keep the oil from spreading. They tried to stop even more oil spilling into the sea.

No one could tell how much of the tanker's load had already been lost. Maybe a quarter of its tanks had already bled into Prince William Sound. That could have been 50 million litres (13 million gallons) of stinking crude oil. It was vital to limit the harm it could cause.

Members of the US Coast Guard helped with the clean-up operation.

CONCERN GROWS

Divers swam beneath the *Exxon Valdez* on Saturday 25 March. According to Frank Iarossi, president of the Exxon Shipping Company, they found the ship in a far less stable position than they first thought. There was real concern that the ship could capsize and release all the remaining oil into the water.

By Sunday 26 March, the clean-up teams were working at full speed. In the afternoon it seemed that no more oil was leaking from the tanker. At last there was hope. But by late afternoon, the skimmers had still only scooped up about 47,000 litres (12,500 gallons). There was much more to remove.

On 26 March the weather was calm and sunny, with the snowy mountains standing bright and clear above the oily water in the bay. But a warning came that the weather would change. Monday's forecast was that waves would be 2 metres (7 feet) high, with winds reaching 40 kilometres (25 miles) per hour. This would make the oil much harder to remove.

The **toxic** slick seeped around tiny Reef Island, about 1 mile (1.6 kilometres) east of the grounded tanker. It crept ashore on the north end of Bligh Island. Like slimy claws, it clung to the rocks. A decision had to be made. It was time to fight back with fire.

The plan was to burn off the oil floating on the sea. The first attempt worked well. A fireproof boom held the slick still as flame-throwers set the oily crust alight. Flames ripped across the surface of the sea. The air became thick with black, choking smoke.

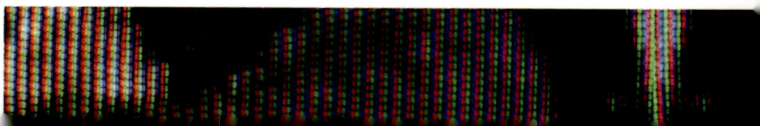

OIL KEEPS SPREADING

"The spill from the tanker *Exxon Valdez* spread its oily fingers over more than 100 square miles of Prince William Sound [by] Sunday, Day 3 of the largest oil spill in the nation's history."

Anchorage Daily News,
27 March 1989

Burning the oil off the sea caused air pollution.

Despite the risk of smoke and flames getting out of control, the first attempt was a success. The fire burnt off some of the slick. More fires were planned for the next morning. At least, that was the plan. "With all the skimmers in the world, we'll never clean up this spill," the Exxon chief said. He told everyone that three different clean-up methods would be used on Monday. They would be chemicals, skimmers, and more fire. However, by Monday the weather had turned for the worse.

CHEMICAL WARFARE

Chemicals called detergents can help to break down crude oil. These **detergents** cause the thick tar that floats on the water to break up and sink. By spraying chemicals over the slick, the clean-up team hoped to **dissolve** a lot of the oil.

Not everyone was happy about spraying chemicals over the slick. Detergents can harm plants and animals. If the oil sank to the seabed, it would choke all underwater life. Even so, it was decided to take the risk and spray the slick in Prince William Sound.

There were three main problems. There was not enough detergent available, there were not enough planes to spray the detergent, and the sea was too calm on the Sunday. Gentle waves were needed to help mix up the sea water, oil, and detergent. The first spray had very little effect. On Monday 27 March the sea became too rough for the detergent to work.

HEAVY SEAS

Three days after the *Exxon Valdez* grounded, a storm pushed more oil on to the rocky shores and the beaches of Knight Island.

Aeroplanes were used to spray chemicals on to the oil in Prince William Sound.

Much of the oil was removed using two fishing boats connected to an oil skimmer by containment booms.

Scooping up the oil and dragging it to shore with booms and skimmers was not easy. Oil-caked seaweed soon clogged up the equipment. The weight of the thick, heavy oil was too much for the skimmers to handle. It took valuable time to fix damaged parts. Time was one thing the now-exhausted workers did not have. The wind began to pick up, the clouds grew darker, and the sea started to swell with an approaching storm.

CLOGGING UP

Skimmers work best in calm water. In rough or choppy sea, skimmers tend to pick up more water than oil. Very thick oil, debris, or ice can cause some types of skimmer to jam. Where pumps are used to suck up the oil into storage tanks, they can easily become clogged. Pumps only work well in calm water.

THE NEXT
FEW DAYS

The *Exxon Valdez*, 1989

THE WEATHER TURNS

On Monday the clean-up work had to stop as strong north-east winds blew across the water.

The oil was whipped into what looked like an ocean of frothy chocolate mousse. All boats had to head for shelter. Aircraft that were used to drop detergent on the oil could not fly in the howling wind. The grounded tanker was now **listing** in the rough sea.

By evening, as the wind started to drop, a few boats headed back to the slick. It was now 800 metres (0.5 miles) wide and 64 kilometres (40 miles) long, and it was still growing. A few aeroplanes took off to drop detergent around Seal Island, 48 kilometres (30 miles) from the tanker. But already beaches had turned black. The threat to wildlife was worse than ever. The real rescue work was yet to start.

Foam sludge polluted the beaches it washed up on.

FIRST CASUALTIES

After just a few days, the bodies of hundreds of animals and birds lay on the slimy beaches. Within a week, currents and winds had pushed the slick nearly 160 kilometres (100 miles) out to sea. In time, creatures as far as 800 kilometres (500 miles) away from the wrecked *Exxon Valdez* became coated with its deadly oil.

Finding all the oil-coated creatures was hard. Taking them away to treat them was another problem. Dealing with sick birds was not easy because:

- the coastline stretched over long distances in a remote, wild, and freezing landscape
- beaches were so rugged that in many places it was not possible to land a boat
- some wild animals were so scared and powerful that they hurt the rescuers trying to help them
- it was so far back to base, where an animal hospital was set up, that many birds died on the journey.

RESCUE PROBLEMS

"Once you catch an oiled bird, you can't leave it in a box for 12 hours. It has to be cleaned up and fed."

A rescue worker

Some workers used spoons to scrape up oil from the beaches.

Rescue workers tried to save birds such as this cormorant that were caked in oil.

The rescue teams began to realize what a difficult and massive job they had to do.

When sea birds get covered in oil they can no longer fly and catch fish to eat. They also swallow poisonous oil when they try to clean themselves with their beaks. Without help the birds die. Even with help, they have to be cleaned, dried, fed, and cared for very quickly.

The rescue team worked flat out to clean oil from the feathers of hundreds of birds. They rushed them back to base for treatment.

HELPLESS

The oil spread west from Valdez to choke and drown the wildlife of Prince William Sound. The rescue team could only watch helplessly as sick creatures struggled and flapped ashore. "A body count of dead animals is about all that anyone can hope to do," said Jon Lyman, of the Alaska Department of Fish and Game.

THE CLEAN-UP OPERATION

Among the casualties were sea otters. They feed on fish and clams in Prince William Sound. Like the birds, otters died from being poisoned, but they also died from cold. The oil got in their fur and stopped it **insulating** their bodies from the cold water. Many other otters were blinded by oil that coated their eyes. About 1,000 dead otters were found over the next weeks and months. Many more must have died at sea and were never found.

Cleaning the otters took a lot of skill. They may look cuddly, but they have sharp teeth and claws. Wild animals in distress do not understand that they are being helped, and are afraid of humans. The **volunteer** helpers had to handle the otters very carefully.

After being washed in soapy water and often tube-fed, many otters survived. But they could only be released back into the wild when the threat had passed, which took many more months of hard work.

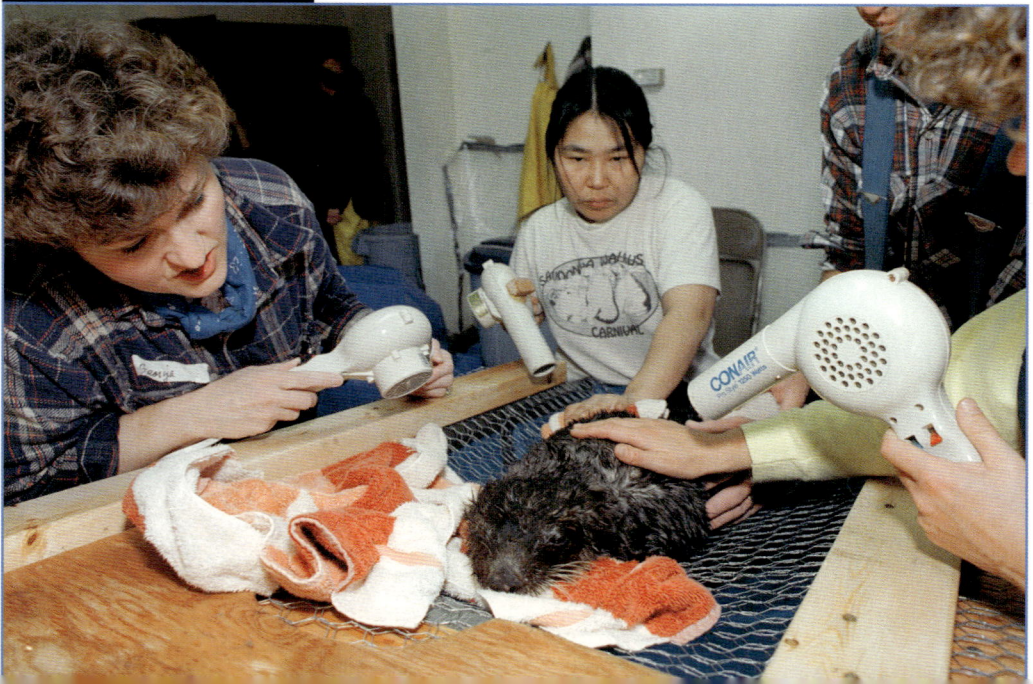

FURTHER DAMAGE

Workers cleaned beaches with high-pressure fire hoses. Hot water shifted the oil, but it also killed small **organisms** and did as much harm as the oil itself in destroying the **habitat**.

Volunteers helped to clean oil from sea otters and other animals.

Workers used high-pressure hot water hoses and pumps to remove oil from the rocks.

It took years for the clean-up operation to deal with all the beaches. Of the 2,100 kilometres (1,300 miles) of coastline that were **contaminated**, about 320 kilometres (200 miles) were badly affected. At its peak, the clean-up effort included 10,000 workers, about 1,000 boats, and around 100 aeroplanes and helicopters. The team was known as "the Exxon army, navy, and air force".

Despite everyone's efforts, a huge area became contaminated. Thousands of creatures died and many beaches remained contaminated for years. In fact, natural forces did most of the cleaning. Waves and winter storms probably did more to clean up the beaches than all the human effort put together.

PAYING THE PRICE

The *Exxon Valdez*, 1989

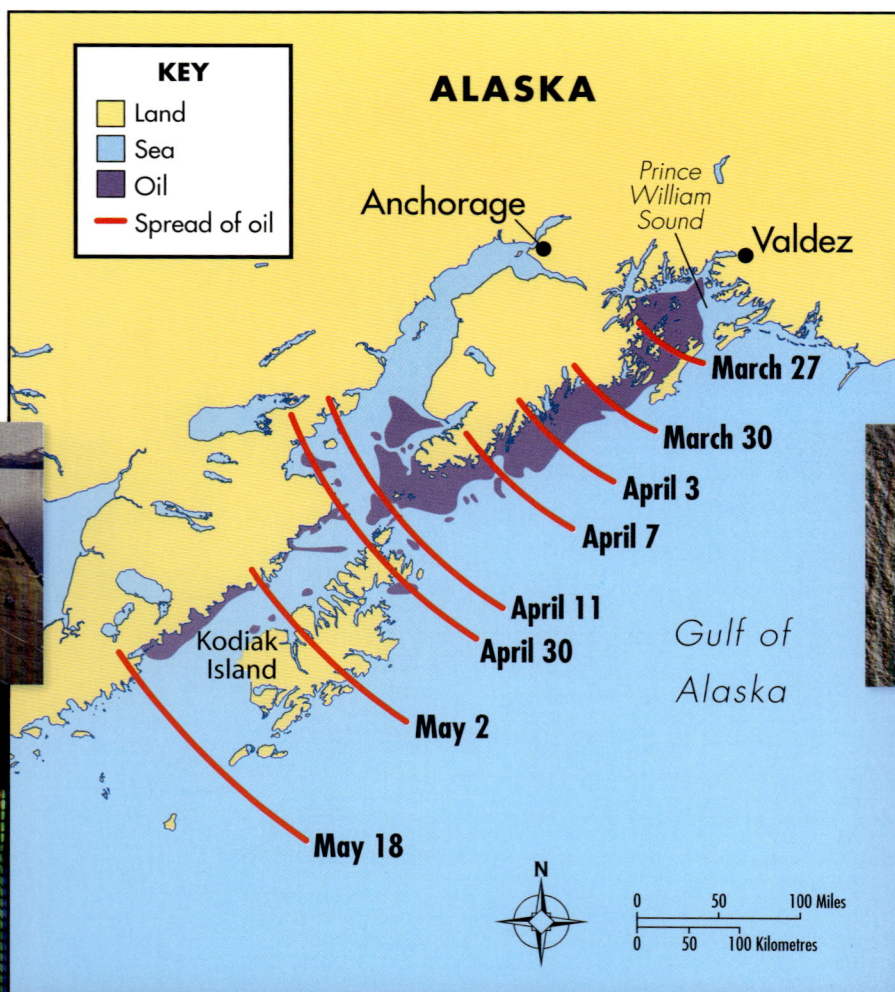

KEY
- Land
- Sea
- Oil
- Spread of oil

ALASKA

Anchorage

Prince William Sound

Valdez

March 27

March 30

April 3

April 7

April 11

April 30

Kodiak Island

May 2

Gulf of Alaska

May 18

N

0   50   100 Miles

0   50   100 Kilometres

LIFE IN THE BALANCE

During the summer of 1989, over 10,000 people worked to clean up the mess left by the *Exxon Valdez*.

Exxon paid them and bought equipment, transport, and food. The town of Valdez grew to three times its normal size as people and money poured in. Exxon spent more than US $2 billion trying to put right the damage caused by the disaster.

After two more summers of work, most of the clean-up crews went home. Nearly everyone who had rushed to Valdez in 1989 had gone by the end of 1991. The following year the State of Alaska and the US Coast Guard declared the clean-up operation was over. But could Prince William Sound ever return to normal?

The crowds had gone but so had millions of creatures. The remains of the oil lay hidden on the beaches and the seabed.

This map shows how quickly the oil spread from the tanker.

THE COST TO THE SEA

It had taken just a few days for the oil to spew into the sea, but it will take decades for Prince William Sound and beyond to recover. The sea and all that lives in it or by it must pay the price for years to come.

The Native Americans of Alaska had farmed and fished the area around Prince William Sound for centuries. The sea gave them their food and their living. They sold what they caught or made from the pure waters around the coast. The **Chugach** people talk of 24 March 1989 as "the day the water died". Many of the salmon, herring, clams, and seals they depended upon were killed. Within two years, many of the Chugach people were **bankrupt**. Many others found it difficult to make a living.

Local residents found dead sea birds for many weeks after the *Exxon Valdez* ran aground.

After the *Exxon Valdez* ran aground, people described the coast as being strangely silent. Birds, **mammals**, fish, and **molluscs** no longer fed along the shore. The fishing industry of the Sound came to a halt. Salmon and herring farms had to close. So did the shrimp, cod, and crab beds. For many years, stocks of fish remained very low.

Most fishing had to stop for the next few years. In 1993, the Pacific herring season in the Sound was cut short because there were so few fish. Four years after the spill, sixty-five fishing boats **blockaded** tanker traffic at Valdez. Fishermen felt they had to protest that catches of wild pink salmon had fallen to an all-time low. This had a major impact on the local **economy**. Very few tourists visited the area, either. Only the oil tankers kept coming, day after day, just like before. The oil still had to be transported to wherever it was needed.

DEATHS

No one really knows the full cost to wildlife, but estimates put deaths at:

- 250,000 seabirds
- 2,800 sea otters
- 300 harbour seals,
- 250 bald eagles
- up to 22 killer whales
- billions of fish eggs.

THE HUMAN COST

For many years people have disagreed about the effects of the *Exxon Valdez* oil spill. Most people agree it was a terrible mistake that caused a major crisis. No one was prepared. Cleaning up the oil took a long time and cost billions of US dollars. Many animals died, and the fishing industry suffered. But some people think this did not become the major disaster everyone feared. After all, no humans died. No one was even badly hurt. The area soon seemed to recover. Wildlife returned. In time the problem went away. Today no one would know where the oil had been. Or would they?

Other people believe the Alaskan environment will never recover. They believe life in the Sound is still suffering from the effects of the disaster, including the people who live near by. They believe that the long-term effects for the workers and locals who breathed the fumes or ate fish caught in the area may never be known.

Many clean-up workers breathed in tiny carbon **particles**, which can harm the lungs. In 1989, 1,811 workers made compensation claims because they said they had breathing problems caused by the clean-up operation. People in a number of towns and villages around Prince William Sound had illnesses related to stress and depression. Doctors believed this was due to the strain of dealing with the disaster.

Fishermen continued to report high levels of stress as a result of the tanker accident. Estimates put the cost to local fishermen from US $6 million to US $43 million in lost business. There were also the stresses of the legal battles when local people claimed for loss of earnings as well as illness. Arguments are still going on. No one will ever know how many forests of paper, millions of hours, and billions of dollars the process has cost.

Workers wore protective clothing and masks while cleaning the oil from the beaches.

ON TRIAL

The *Exxon Valdez, 1989*

THE FATE OF THE EXXON VALDEZ

The story of the *Exxon Valdez* angered many people – this disaster should never have happened.

Those responsible for the disaster had to be punished. Nothing like this should ever happen again. The courts and lawyers were ready.

Just over a week after she ran aground, the *Exxon Valdez* was re-floated off Bligh Reef. She was later towed to San Diego, California, where she was repaired. Around 1,600 tons of steel was removed and replaced at a cost of US $30 million. A year later the tanker was renamed *SeaRiver Mediterranean*, and she put to sea again. The tanker was banned by law from going anywhere near Prince William Sound ever again. Today she carries oil across the Atlantic.

The Exxon Shipping Company was given a new name, too. It is now known as the SeaRiver Shipping Company.

The *Exxon Valdez* was towed out of Prince William Sound by a tug boat and the US Coast Guard.

CAPTAIN IN THE DOCK

At the start of 1990, the world watched as the case of the *Exxon Valdez* came to court. The full story had to be heard in front of a judge and jury. It would take months to hear every detail and find out why the disaster happened, who was to blame, and who should be punished. It would take years to agree who should pay for all the damage, how much, and to whom.

The captain was the only person charged as a result of the spill. The three charges against him were:

- being drunk in charge of a water craft
- causing danger by being **reckless**
- causing a **negligent** discharge of oil.

If found guilty, he faced being sent to prison for 7 years and being fined over US $60,000.

HAZELWOOD TRIAL BEGINS

"The outrage and passion unleashed by the nation's largest oil spill settled into an Anchorage courtroom today in a trial that will determine if Captain Joe Hazelwood or anyone else answers for the wreck of the *Exxon Valdez*."

*Anchorage Daily News,
29 January 1990*

Large numbers of journalists and photographers followed the court case.

The Alaskan courtroom was very tense. Had the captain been drunk? It was a serious charge. He had been seen in a bar in Valdez on the night of the accident. A blood test later showed that he had been drinking. The full story was told of the night when the tanker ran aground. A tape of the captain's message to the coastguard was played. After nearly 2 months, it was time for the jury's **verdict**. Everyone waited in silence. The reporters sat patiently, their pens scribbling on their notepads.

For the first charge, the jury gave its verdict: not guilty. There were murmurs across the court. For the second charge the jury also found Hazelwood not guilty. People were amazed. Then came the third charge. The reply was loud and clear: guilty.

Captain Joseph Hazelwood was fined US $50,000 and sentenced to 1,000 hours of community service in Alaska. He never worked for Exxon again.

HAZELWOOD TALKS

"Am I ridden with guilt? No. Am I feeling responsible as a professional? Well, whether it's a mechanical failure or anything else that grounds you, it sucks."

Joseph Hazelwood

Joseph Hazelwood had to perform community service at Bean's Cafe, a hostel for the homeless.

LEGAL BATTLES

If the oil spill itself wasn't messy enough, all the court cases that followed made it an even messier business. Many lawyers grew rich from the *Exxon Valdez* oil spill. Even today some people complain that Exxon has not paid up fully for the cost of the disaster. Other people complain that only a small number of people who sued Exxon were paid. They say that just a few people received large sums of money to make up for their suffering. Newspapers called them "spillionaires".

Exxon claimed it paid about US $300 million to fishermen for the losses they suffered. It also spent US $2 billion cleaning up the spill and paid US $1 billion to settle other claims. The company was made to pay another US $5 billion in 1994, although this verdict has been under appeal since then. Many people argue that Exxon has not had to pay out very much because its **insurance** company paid many of the bills.

TAKEN TO COURT

"The state of Alaska filed its long awaited lawsuit Tuesday against Exxon and the owners of the trans-Alaska pipeline, charging they grossly deceived the public about their ability to move crude oil safely, or to clean it up when they failed."

Anchorage Daily News,
16 August 1989

Ten years after the disaster, protesters took to the streets of Anchorage to complain that more still had to be done.

BIG OIL - BIG LIES:
THE EXXON DISASTER CONTINUES

Criminal Plea Agreement $ 150 $ MILLION DOLLARS

This diagram shows where some of the payments went.

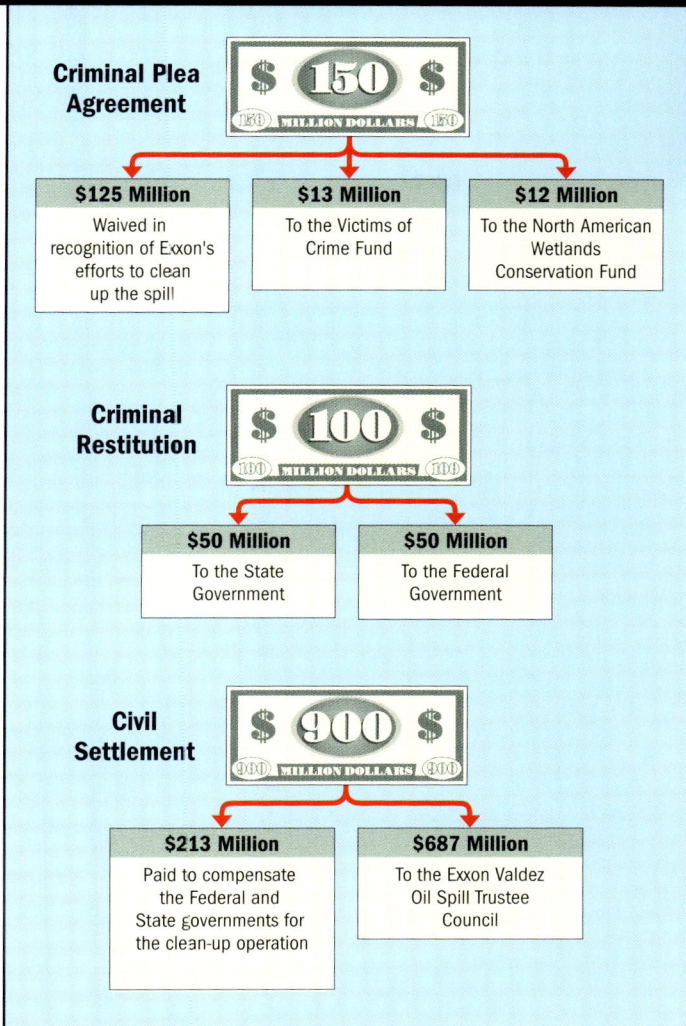

$125 Million	$13 Million	$12 Million
Waived in recognition of Exxon's efforts to clean up the spill	To the Victims of Crime Fund	To the North American Wetlands Conservation Fund

Criminal Restitution $ 100 $ MILLION DOLLARS

$50 Million	$50 Million
To the State Government	To the Federal Government

Civil Settlement $ 900 $ MILLION DOLLARS

$213 Million	$687 Million
Paid to compensate the Federal and State governments for the clean-up operation	To the Exxon Valdez Oil Spill Trustee Council

Exxon was fined US $150 million, the largest fine ever charged for an environmental crime. The court forgave US $125 million of that fine because Exxon had paid to clean up the spill. Of the remaining US $25 million, US $12 million went to the North American Wetlands Conservation Fund and US $13 million went to the national Victims of Crime Fund.

As a direct result of the *Exxon Valdez* disaster, the law was changed in the United States. In 1990, the Oil Pollution Act was brought in to stop further oil spills happening in the United States.

THE OIL POLLUTION ACT

"A company cannot ship oil into the United States until it presents a plan to prevent spills that may occur. It must also have a detailed containment and clean-up plan in case of an oil spill emergency."

YEARS LATER

The *Exxon Valdez, 1989*

COULD IT HAVE BEEN WORSE?

Disasters remain real to everyone involved for years after they occur.

Disasters may no longer make headlines or appear on television but many people have to live with the memories and long-term effects. For some people, life is never the same again.

Despite the terrible effects of the *Exxon Valdez* disaster on the environment, wildlife, and people's jobs, it could have been far worse. The tanker could have rolled over or exploded. Far more of its oil could have escaped. Lives could have been lost or people could have been badly hurt.

The skill of rescue workers prevented this accident being much worse. In fact, the *Exxon Valdez* may even be remembered for causing new laws to be made, which should make the future safer.

Experts thought the oil would be gone by 1995, but oil was still present in 2004 – 15 years after the spill.

THE COST CONTINUES

Living things depend on each other. There is often a fine balance in the way different **species** live together. Tiny creatures are eaten by larger ones, and they in turn are eaten by even bigger animals. But a **food chain** can soon break down. Then many creatures suffer and can disappear in an area forever. This is what happened when oil from the *Exxon Valdez* began to kill marine life in Prince William Sound. People were also in danger. Anyone eating fish from Alaska ran the risk of getting harmful chemicals into their bodies.

The effects on the **ecosystem** will last for a long time. Sea otters and ducks continued to die from eating contaminated food for years after the accident. The sea, wind, and rain have now been cleaning the oily Alaskan shores for many years. There has been a lot of recovery. But for some species there is a long way to go. Another oil spill in Prince William Sound could damage the ecosystem forever.

A FINE BALANCE

Each living thing within an ecosystem depends on other living things. For example, when the fish died in Prince William Sound there was less food for the seals that normally eat them. As those seals died there was less food for the killer whales that eat seals.

Animals today are still suffering the consequences of the *Exxon Valdez* oil spill.

Gray whales were the largest casualties of the oil spill.

As long as the world demands oil, our planet will always be at risk. Finding, shipping, and burning oil cause much pollution. The *Exxon Valdez* disaster is a reminder that our planet is under threat from oil. The following warning was given to the US **Senate** soon after the disaster:

"SO FEW CAN DESTROY SO MUCH"

"It doesn't take a disaster to destroy wilderness. The hundreds of miles of pipelines, roads, docks, airstrips, the thousands of workers, the constant roar of trucks, planes, and the drilling equipment itself destroy the wilderness even if it is carried on with care...

We all mourn for Prince William Sound and the life that is no more. And it is also common to feel anger. Anger over broken promises. Anger over lies. Anger over greed. Anger that so few can destroy so much. Let us protect our wild places, our last wild places, from ever being victims of another disaster."

Michael Fisher, Sierra Club (an environmental organization).

LESSONS LEARNED

Some people see the *Exxon Valdez* disaster as a wake-up call. It showed what damage an oil spill can do, and raised many questions about how to prepare for future disasters.

Although the accident destroyed so much, a great deal was learned. The oil industry had to make changes. Another *Exxon Valdez* disaster must never happen again. Because Valdez was just not ready to deal with an accident on such a scale, today there are many new rules in place:

- the US Coast Guard now monitors full tankers via satellite as they pass through Prince William Sound
- two boats escort each tanker as it passes through the sound. They not only watch over the tankers, but they can help in an emergency such as a loss of power.
- trained sea pilots, with much experience in Prince William Sound, go on board all tankers from a new pilot station at Bligh Reef. They now steer each ship for 40 kilometres (25 miles).

The port of Valdez, and the rest of the oil industry, are now better prepared to deal with oil spills.

Biologists continue to study animals to check for lasting damage from the oil.

Five more lessons were learned that brought important changes to Alaska:

- a new law requires all tankers using Prince William Sound to be **double-hulled** by 2015. It is believed that the *Exxon Valdez* would have lost less than half the amount of oil if it had had a double-hull.
- planning for oil spills in Prince William Sound is now part of regular US Coast Guard training. Local fishing fleets and state of Alaska employees are also trained to respond quickly to an oil spill. In 1989 much time was lost because of poor planning and training.
- modern skimmers can now remove 10 times more oil from water than those used in 1989. Even if more oil could have been skimmed up in 1989, there would have been nowhere to put it. Today, there is emergency storage space for more than 95 million litres (25 million gallons) of recovered oil.
- there are now 64 kilometres (40 miles) of booms in Prince William Sound. This is seven times the amount available at the time of the *Exxon Valdez* spill.
- detergents are now stockpiled for use. Helicopters, aeroplanes, and boats are ready to spray them very quickly.

Because of the lessons learned in 1989, the risk of another oil spill in Alaska should be far lower today.

DID YOU KNOW?

The US government bought 236,000 hectares (650,000 acres) of forest and coastal land to protect the animals that live near Prince William Sound. The recovery of these areas will not be disturbed by either humans or pollution. Scientists can use the land to learn more about the area's ecosystem.

47

NEVER AGAIN?

Every year since the *Exxon Valdez* ran aground on underwater rocks, an oil spill has happened somewhere in the world. A few of the recent oil spills are listed on pages 50 and 51. Some tankers still clean their tanks **illegally** by flushing out their oily sludge into the sea. Others have caught fire or even sunk. Massive supertankers are not easy to control. Some tankers take up to 3 kilometres (2 miles) to slow down and stop. Even with the latest equipment, they can still crash or run aground. Human error could cause another disaster like the *Exxon Valdez* oil spill.

When environmental disasters strike in remote areas, some people are not worried. Some people may not think it very serious if only an empty stretch of water, some quiet beaches, and a few animals are harmed.

The beautiful Alaskan landscape is still at risk from pollution.

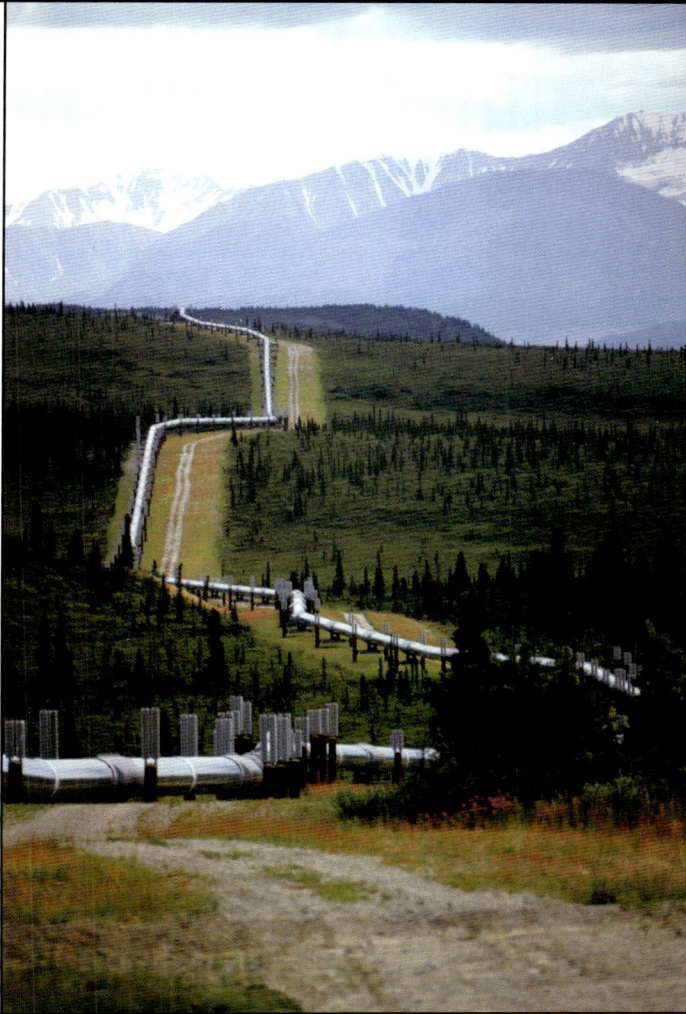

The trans-Alaska pipeline carries oil across the landscape for 1300 kilometres (800 miles).

But one day it might be their beach that gets polluted, their food that becomes poisoned, and their jobs that are affected. How would they feel if the next supertanker to poison the sea was close to their home? How would you feel if it happened near you?

Many people care deeply about looking after life on Earth. Unless we protect the natural world, future generations will never see many of the creatures that still share our planet. That is why we should never let another disaster like the *Exxon Valdez* oil spill happen again.

TIMELINE

Some of the largest oil spills from tankers in the last 40 years:

1967 The *Torrey Canyon* spills 144.6 million litres (38.2 million gallons) near Cornwall, England.

1968 The *Mandoil* spills 47.7 million litres (12.6 million gallons) near the United States.

1969 The *Julius Schindler* spills 107.5 million litres (28.4 million gallons) near Portugal.

1970 The *Othello* spills 68.9 million litres (18.2 million gallons) near Sweden.

1971 The *Wafra* spills 76.5 million litres (20.2 million gallons) near South Africa.

1972 The *Sea Star* spills 143.5 million litres (37.9 million gallons) near the Gulf of Oman.

1975 The *Jakob Maersk* spills 92 million litres (24.3 million gallons) near Portugal.

1975 The *Epic Colocotronis* spills 68.1 million litres (18 million gallons) in the Caribbean Sea.

1976 The *Urquiola* spills 106.4 million litres (28.1 million gallons) near Spain.

1976 The *St. Peter* spills 39 million litres (10.3 million gallons) near Colombia.

1977 The *Hawaiian Patriot* spills 118.1 million litres (31.2 million gallons) near Hawaii.

1978 The *Amoco Cadiz* spills 260.1 million litres (68.7 million gallons) near France.

1978 The *Andros Patria* spills 55.3 million litres (14.6 million gallons) near Spain.

1979 The *Atlantic Express* spills 157.1 million litres (41.5 million gallons) near Barbados.

1979 The *Burmah Agate* spills 40.5 million litres (10.7 million gallons) near the United States.

1979 The *Gino* spills 38.2 million litres (10.1 million gallons) near France.

1980 The *Irenes Serenade* spills 138.6 million litres (36.6 million gallons) near Greece.

1983 The *Castillo de Bellver* spills 297.2 million litres (78.5 million gallons) near South Africa.

1985 The *Nova* spills 81 million litres (21.4 million gallons) near Iran.

1988 The *Odyssey* spills 163.2 million litres (43.1 million gallons) near Canada.

1988 The *Athenian Venture* spills 40.1 million litres (10.6 million gallons) near Canada.

1989 The *Exxon Valdez* spills 41.6 million litres (11 million gallons) near Alaska, United States.

1991 The *Haven* spills 159 million litres (42 million gallons) near Italy.

1991 The *ABT Summer* spills 57.5 million litres (15.2 million gallons) near Angola.

1992 The *Aegean Sea* spills 82.9 million litres (21.9 million gallons) near Spain.

1992 The *Katina P.* spills 56.8 million litres (15 million gallons) near South Africa.

1993 The *Braer* spills 94.6 million litres (25 million gallons) near Scotland.

1994 The *Thanassis A.* spills 40.9 million litres (10.8 million gallons) near Hong Kong.

1996 The *Sea Empress* spills 80.6 million litres (21.3 million gallons) near South Wales.

2002 The *Prestige* spills 75.7 million litres (20 million gallons) near Spain.

GLOSSARY

Alaska Response Team group of experts who respond to pollution incidents in Alaska

bankrupt person who has run out of money and is unable to pay any bills

blockade cutting off an area to stop the coming in or going out of people or supplies

boom line of connected floating timbers used to catch objects floating on the sea

bridge part of the boat from where the captain controls it

capsize when a boat overturns

Chugach group of Alaskan Native Americans

contaminate make impure or unfit for use

deep-water skimmer machine used to remove oil from water

detergent soapy chemical that cleans

dissolve mix with water and break up or disappear

double-hulled method of building an oil tanker that makes the ship less likely to lose oil if it runs aground

economy use of money and goods, for example buying and selling

ecosystem a place and the living things in it

environment surrounding conditions, such as soil, climate, and plants that affect the survival of life

food chain series of living things in which each eats the next smallest member of the series

grounded a grounded ship is one that has become stuck on the sea bed and unable to move

habitat place where a plant or animal normally lives or grows

helmsman officer on a ship who is responsible for steering it

illegal against the law

insulated protected against heat-loss

insurance guarantee of payment for the value of property if it is lost or damaged

listing leaning to one side

mammal warm-blooded animal that is not a reptile, fish, or bird; almost all mammals give birth to live young

mollusc soft-bodied animal, often with a shell, such as a clam or a mussel

negligent failing to take proper care of something

oil field area rich in oil deposits in the rock

oil slick layer of oil that has been spilt on the surface of the sea

organism living plant or animal

particle small amount of something that cannot be seen without a microscope

pollution spoiling the environment with dangerous chemicals, fumes, or rubbish

reckless being careless and showing lack of caution

reef chain of rocks or ridge of sand just below the surface of the water

rudder moving flap attached to the rear of a ship or aeroplane that is used for steering

Senate upper house of US Congress, where government makes the laws of the land

ship's log instrument that records a ship's speed and course

sound narrow passage of water that often forms a channel between the mainland and an island

species group of animals and plants whose members share most features

starboard if you face the front of a ship, starboard is the right-hand side of the ship

third mate junior officer on a ship, usually the safety officer

toxic poisonous

verdict decision made by a jury in court

volunteer person who freely offers to help

FINDING OUT MORE

BOOKS

Designed for Success: Superboats, Ian Graham (Heinemann Library, 2003)

Energy Essentials: Fossil Fuels, Steven Chapman (Raintree, 2004)

Environmental Disasters: The Exxon Valdez Oil Spill, Elspeth Leacock (Facts on File, 2005)

Green Alert: Threatened Habitat, Uma Sachidhanandam (Raintree, 2004)

Mean Machines: Boats, Mark Morris (Raintree, 2004)

New Energy Sources, Nigel Hawkes (Franklin Watts, 2000)

You Can Save the Planet: Clean Planet: Stopping Litter and Pollution, Tristan Boyer Binns (Heinemann Library, 2005)

EXXON VALDEZ ONLINE

www.evostc.state.ak.us/
The Oil Spill Trustee Council are involved in the restoration of the environment affected by the *Exxon Valdez* disaster.

www.soc.soton.ac.uk/CHD/classroom@sea/general_science/oil_cleanup.html
This Classroom@Sea page has more information about how oil spills are cleaned up.

www.reefed.edu.au

The Reef Guardian Schools Program work to help keep the Great Barrier Reef clean.

www.georesources.co.uk/oilspill.htm

Go to this site to learn facts about major oil tanker accidents and spills.

response.restoration.noaa.gov/photos/ships/ships.html

Look at more photographs of oil spills from around the world.

www.foei.org

The website of Friends of the Earth, with lots of information about projects and campaigns

www.environment-agency.gov.uk

The Environment Agency's website contains information about many different issues.

FURTHER RESEARCH:

If you are interested in finding out more about oil spills, try researching the following topics on the internet or at your local library:

- the *Torrey Canyon* disaster
- the world oil trade
- Alaska's wildlife.

INDEX

Titles in the *When Disaster Struck* series include:

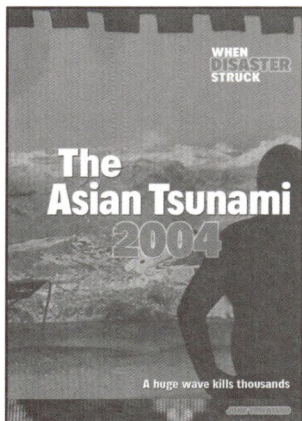

WHEN DISASTER STRUCK

The Asian Tsunami 2004

A huge wave kills thousands

Hardback   1 406 20291 6

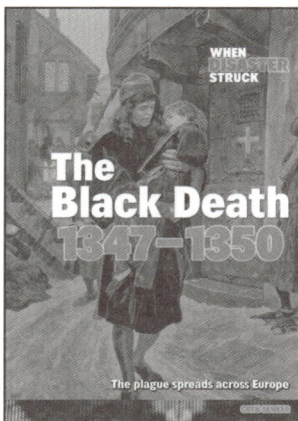

WHEN DISASTER STRUCK

The Black Death 1347–1350

The plague spreads across Europe

Hardback   1 406 20286 X

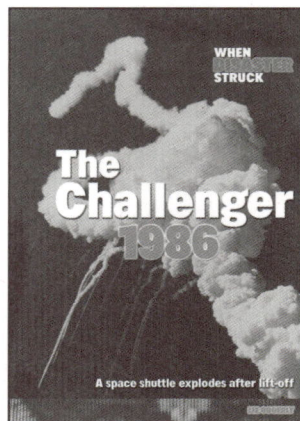

WHEN DISASTER STRUCK

The Challenger 1986

A space shuttle explodes after lift-off

Hardback   1 406 20287 8

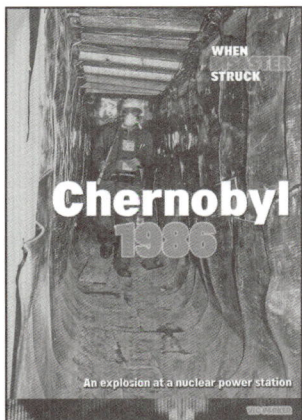

WHEN DISASTER STRUCK

Chernobyl 1986

An explosion at a nuclear power station

Hardback   1 406 20285 1

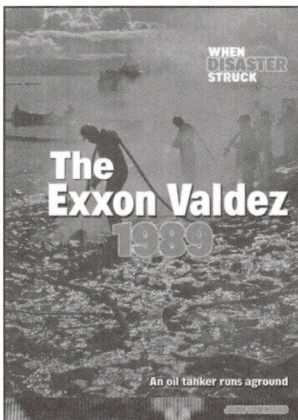

WHEN DISASTER STRUCK

The Exxon Valdez 1989

An oil tanker runs aground

Hardback   1 406 20292 4

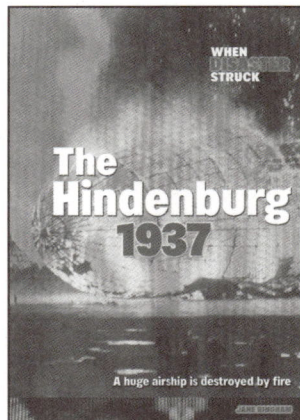

WHEN DISASTER STRUCK

The Hindenburg 1937

A huge airship is destroyed by fire

Hardback   1 406 20293 2

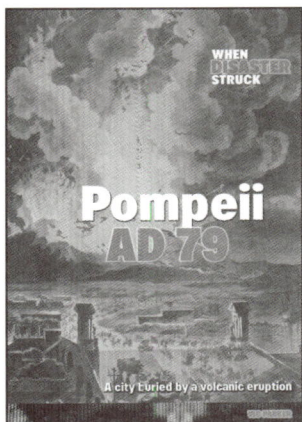

WHEN DISASTER STRUCK

Pompeii AD 79

A city buried by a volcanic eruption

Hardback   1 406 20290 8

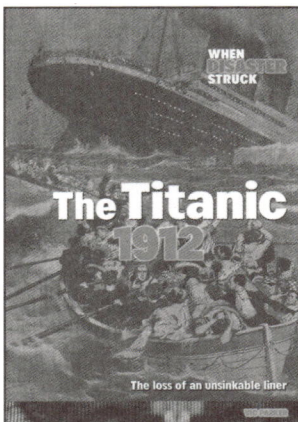

WHEN DISASTER STRUCK

The Titanic 1912

The loss of an unsinkable liner

Hardback   1 406 20288 6

Find out about other titles from Raintree on our website www.raintreepublishers.co.uk